Introduction

The *Cambridge Primary Science* series has been developed to match the Cambridge International Examinations Primary Science curriculum framework. It is a fun, flexible and easy-to-use course that gives both learners and teachers the support they need. In keeping with the aims of the curriculum itself, it encourages learners to be actively engaged with the content, and develop enquiry skills as well as subject knowledge.

This Activity Book for Stage 6 is designed to be used alongside the Learner's Book for the same stage, ISBN 978-1-107-69980-9.

In this book you will find an exercise to accompany each topic presented in the Learner's Book, as well as a language review exercise at the end of each unit to practise the key vocabulary. The exercises are designed to be completed as pen-and-paper exercises, and learners can work on them individually or in pairs or small groups. The exercises may be set as in-class work or homework.

There are different styles of exercise throughout to maintain interest and to suit different purposes. The main aims of the exercises in this book are:

- to consolidate the subject knowledge presented in the Learner's Book
- to encourage learners to apply this knowledge in new situations, thus developing understanding
- to practise scientific language
- to develop scientific enquiry skills such as presenting and interpreting results from investigations.

The answers to the exercises in this Activity Book are available in the Teacher's Resource Book for Stage 6, ISBN 978-1-107-66202-5. This resource also contains extensive guidance on all the topics, ideas for classroom activities and guidance notes on all the activities presented in the Learner's Book. You will also find a large collection of worksheets.

We hope you enjoy using this series.

With best wishes,
the Cambridge Primary Science team.

Contents

Useful words

active	busy doing things
	Maria is **active** in helping to plan the class party.
affect	to do something that causes a change
	The amount of rain will **affect** how well the crops grow.
check	to make sure that something is correct
	Raoul will **check** his mathematics calculations before he gives them to his teacher to mark.
collect	to find and bring things together
	Kioni will **collect** all the eggs from the hens' nests.
compare	to look at two or more different things and decide how similar or different they are to each other
	Mrs Kahn will **compare** the prices of different brands of tea to see which is the cheapest.
decide	to take action according to available information
	Liam must **decide** whether to take a sun hat after he has seen the weather forecast.
effect	the way in which an event, action or person makes something change
	The **effect** of the rain was a good crop of maize.

explore	to investigate something in depth
	The prince will **explore** all the pathways through the forest until he finds the one that leads to the castle.
evaluate	to compare results or explanations to find the most useful or worthwhile
	Thakane compared her drawing with Vusi's and Thandi's to **evaluate** how good the drawing was.
evidence	signs that show you that something exists or is true
	The footprints were **evidence** that someone had walked in the mud.
factor	something that has an effect on other things
	Rain is a **factor** that could stop the soccer match.
identify	to recognise something in a picture or description and be able to give it a name
	Kaleb was able to **identify** seven parts of the body shown in a diagram.
list	to write down examples as single words with no sentences
	Petra must write a **list** of things she needs to buy at the supermarket.
plan	to think and talk about how you will do something before you carry it out
	The De Sousa family made a **plan** of all the places they would like to visit on their holiday.

Useful words

re-arrange — to change the order of things

Andrew decided to **re-arrange** the flowers in the vase to make them look more attractive.

repeat — to do or say something again

The choir was told to **repeat** the last part of the song until they sang it correctly.

separate — to divide or split something into different parts

Abuya needs to **separate** eggs into egg yolks and egg whites when she bakes a cake.

sort — to put things into groups according to their type

Mr Motswiri needs to **sort** the dirty washing into white clothes and coloured clothes before washing them.

suggest — to introduce the idea of doing something

It looks as though it's going to rain so I **suggest** you take your raincoat.

test — to try something out to see if it works

Naomi plugged in her new electric kettle to **test** whether it worked.

Humans and animals

Exercise 1.1   Body organs

In this exercise, you will name body organs and identify their position in the body.

1   Some body organs are shown. Write the name of the body organ below each drawing.

2   Draw a line from each organ to its correct position in the body.

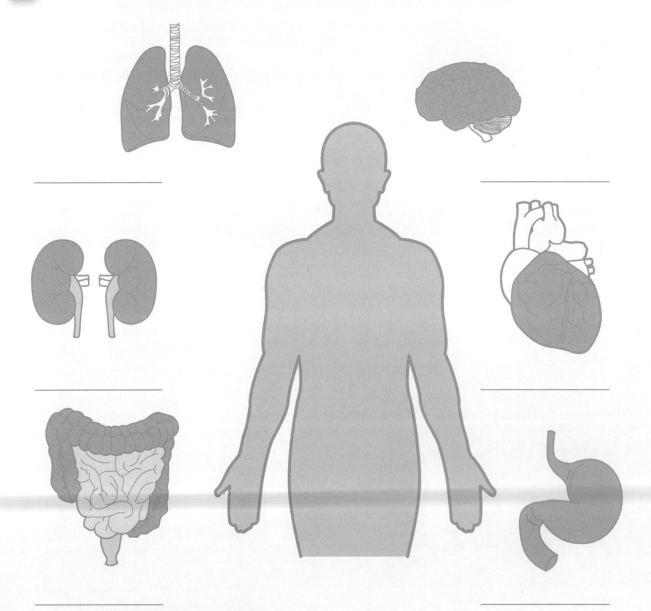

Exercise 1.2　The heart

In this exercise, you will test your knowledge about the heart.

1　a　Name the body system that the heart is part of.

_____

　　　b　Name the **two** other parts of this system.

_____

_____

2　Use the words in the box to complete the sentences. You will need to use some words more than once.

blood　blood vessels　food　lungs　oxygen　waste products

　　　a　The heart pumps _____ through the body.

　　　b　The left side of the heart pumps _____ that contains

　　　　_____.

　　　c　The right side of the heart pumps _____ without _____

　　　　to the _____.

　　　d　Blood is carried in _____.

　　　e　Blood carries _____ and _____ to all parts

　　　　of the body and takes away _____.

Heartbeat and pulse

In this exercise, you will analyse pulse rate measurements.

Name	Pulse rate
Marcus	88
Cui	110
Clara	90
Marta	87
Thabo	90

Marcus and his friends measured their pulse rates. These are their results.

1 What units do we use to measure pulse rate?

_____

2 What is the average pulse rate of the group? How did you work this out?

_____

_____

3 a What pattern can you see in the results?

_____

b Which result does not fit the pattern? Suggest a reason for this.

_____

c How can you find out if your suggestion is correct?

_____

The lungs and breathing

In this exercise, you will make a drawing of the lungs.

1 The drawing shows the lungs when you breathe out.
Make a drawing to show what happens to the lungs when you breathe in.
Label your drawing.

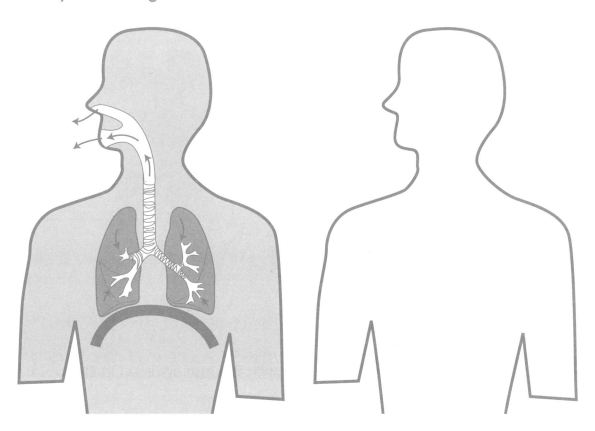

2 Complete the flow diagram using these words to show the oxygen pathway when we breathe in.

| blood | lungs | nose | windpipe |

_____ → _____ → _____ → _____

Exercise 1.5 The digestive system

In this exercise, you will identify the parts of the digestive system and their functions.

1 Label the diagram of the digestive system. Use these words to help you.

> gullet   intestine   mouth   stomach

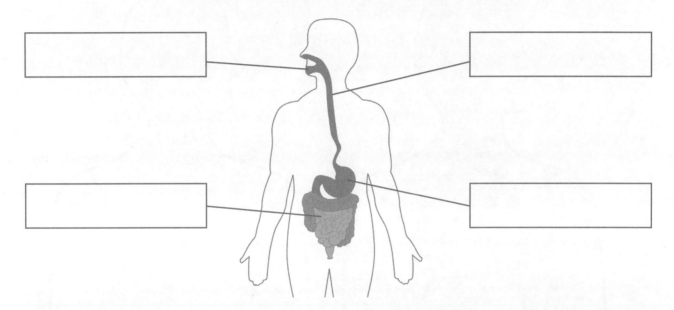

2 a Match each of the labelled parts with its function listed in the table. Write the name of the part next to its function.

Part	Function
	pushes food into the stomach
	mixes food with digestive juices
	chews food and starts digestion
	breaks food down into very tiny particles

b The functions in the table are not in the same order as they happen in the body. Write the functions in the correct order.

_____ → _____ → _____ → _____

Exercise 1.6 What do the kidneys do?

In this exercise, you will complete sentences about the kidneys and their functions.

Use the words in the box to help you. You will need to use some words more than once.

| bean-shaped dialysis disease excretion filter |
| urine waste products water |

The kidneys are a pair of _____ organs. Their main

function is _____. They _____

the blood to remove _____. They also help control the

amount of _____ in the body. The wastes from the

kidneys leave the body as liquid _____. We should drink

enough _____ every day to keep the kidneys healthy.

The kidneys cannot work properly if we have a kidney

_____. Some people need a special machine called a

_____ machine to do the job of the kidneys.

What does the brain do?

This exercise tests your knowledge about the brain.

1 a   Which body system is the brain part of?

_____

  b   Name another part of this body system.

_____

2 Name **two** important body functions that are controlled by the brain without you having to think about them.

_____

_____

3 Choose the part of the brain in the drawing that controls each of the following:

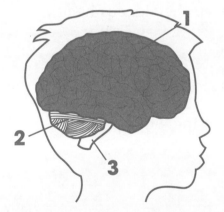

  a   Saying your name _____

  b   Standing on one leg _____

  c   Kicking a ball _____

  d   Listening to music _____

  e   Breathing faster while running

_____

4 Explain why someone who has had a serious head injury may not be able to talk anymore.

_____

_____

_____

Language review

This exercise checks that you understand the scientific words used in this unit.

Choose the correct words from the word box to complete the sentences.

breathing   circulation   circulatory system   controls

digestion   disease   excretion   lungs   nervous system

organs   pulse   urine   windpipe

_____ inside our bodies do different jobs to keep us alive

and healthy.

The pumping of blood around the body is called _____.

The heart, blood vessels and blood form the _____

_____.

Your _____ tells you how fast your heart is beating.

The mouth, stomach and intestines carry out the process of _____.

We take air into our bodies and let air out of our bodies by

_____.

Air moves from the nose, down the _____ and into the

_____.

The main function of the kidneys is _____. They produce a liquid

called _____.

A sickness that stops our bodies working properly is called a

_____.

The brain is part of the _____. It _____ all our

body functions.

Living things in the environment

Exercise 2.1 Food chains in a local habitat

In this exercise, you will apply and practise what you know about habitats and food chains.

This garden is full of plants and animals that live together. The peach tree provides a home and food for the birds and the caterpillars. The roses provide food for the bees and aphids. The grass provides food for ants.

1 Identify the habitat in the picture.

_____

2 Draw **five** food chains to represent the feeding relationships between plants and animals that you can see in the picture.

_____

_____

_____

_____

3 Describe **two** other ways in which plants and animals depend on each other in this garden.

_____

_____

Exercise 2.2 Food chains begin with plants

In this exercise, you will identify producers and consumers and draw a food chain.

Look at this picture.

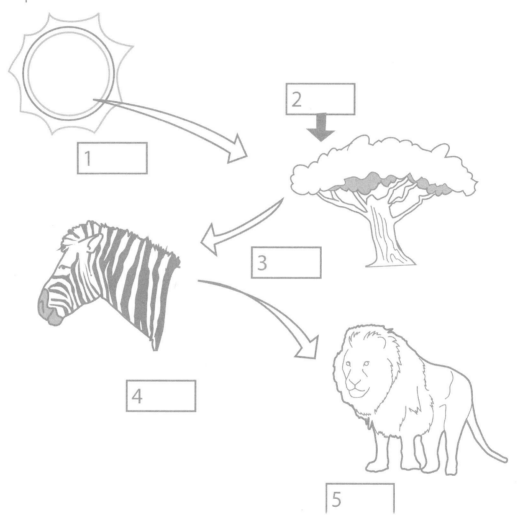

Arrows 1 and 2 represent factors that the tree needs to make food.

1 What does arrow 1 represent?

_____

2 What does arrow 2 represent?

_____

3 What is the third factor that the tree needs to make food?

_____

4 Identify which of the labels 3, 4 and 5 show producers and which show consumers.

a 3 is a _____

b 4 is a _____

c 5 is a _____

5 Draw a food chain to show the feeding relationships in the picture.

In this exercise, you identify predators and their prey, and draw food chains.

Use the drawing to answer these questions.

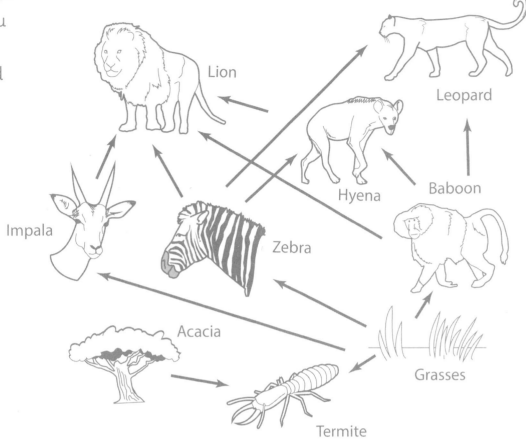

1 Name the **two** producers.

_____

_____

2 Name **four** animals that eat plants.

_____

_____

_____

_____

3 Name **three** predators.

_____

_____

_____

4 Draw **one** food chain with a producer, a prey and a predator.

5 Draw **one** food chain with a producer, a prey and two predators.

Food chains in the Namib Desert

In this exercise, you will analyse and draw food chains in a desert habitat.

The Namib Desert extends for over 1000 km along the coast of Namibia in southern Africa. The Atlantic Ocean is next to the coastline. Very little rain falls in the Namib Desert. Most of the moisture needed by plants comes in the form of mist from the sea.

Many animals live on the sand dunes of the desert. Ants, beetles, beetle larvae and termites eat seeds and bits of dried grass that wind carries from the coast.

The ants are eaten by ant lions, spiders eat termites, and scorpions eat beetle larvae and spiders. Sunspiders eat scorpions, beetles and beetle larvae. Lizards then eat spiders, beetles and sunspiders. The sidewinding adder eats lizards.

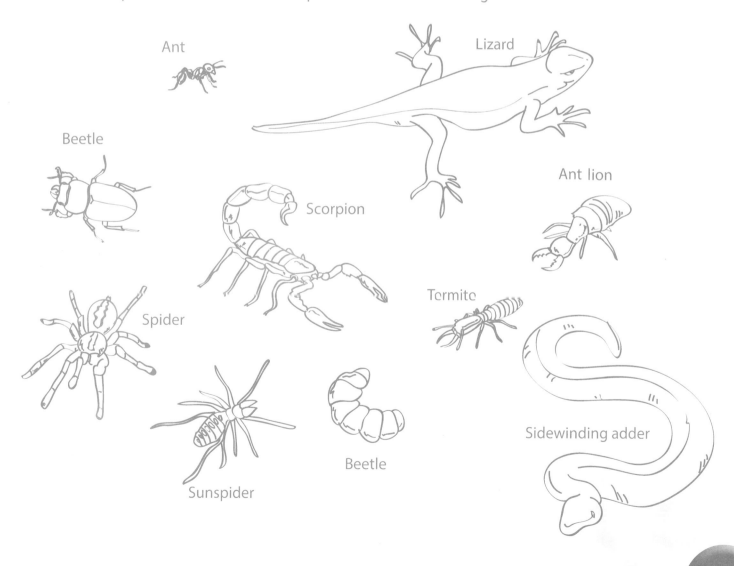

Ant

Lizard

Beetle

Ant lion

Scorpion

Spider

Termite

Sidewinding adder

Sunspider

Beetle

1 a Identify **two** producers in the desert habitat.

_____

_____

b How do these producers get water?

_____

2 Name **three** animals that only eat plants.

_____

_____

_____

3 List **two** predators and their prey.

predator _____ prey _____

predator _____ prey _____

4 Draw **one** food chain with a producer and three consumers to illustrate this habitat.

Exercise 2.5 Deforestation

In this exercise, you will compare different opinions on deforestation.

Read what these people have to say about deforestation:

biologist — If we remove the forest, many kinds of plants and animals will disappear for ever.

carpenter — I need this wood to make tables and chairs.

doctor — There may be new cures for diseases in these trees.

coffee farmer — I can make lots of money from this land planting coffee.

woman with wood — I need this firewood to cook our food.

traditional healer — I need roots and bark from these trees to make my medicines.

logger — I can make good money selling this wood.

old man — The forest provides me with food. What will I eat if they take away the forest?

city planner — The city is expanding, we need to clear more land.

scientist — To stop global warming we have to stop destroying our forests.

Who is in favour of deforestation and who is against it? Fill in this table.

Those in favour of deforestation	Those against deforestation

Exercise 2.6 Air pollution

In this exercise, apply your knowledge about air pollution.

1 Name **three** gases that are polluting cities.

_____

_____

_____

2 What produces each of these pollutants?

_____

_____

_____

3 The most polluted cities are all very large cities with many people living and working in them. Power stations and industries burn coal. How do these factors affect pollution in these cities?

_____

_____

_____

_____

_____

_____

_____

_____

_____

_____

Exercise 2.7 Acid rain

In this exercise, you will apply what you know about acid rain and food chains to a freshwater habitat.

A freshwater lake is a habitat for plants and animals. They depend on one another. Acid rain has a bad effect on this habitat. The plants begin to die. The eggs of fish and amphibians, like frogs and toads, become damaged and may not hatch. Animals such as freshwater shrimps have a tough shell formed of calcium. The acid wears away the calcium and the animal dies.

When one living thing is killed by the acidity in the water, others are affected. For example, fish eat shrimps and herons eat fish. So, if the shrimps die, there will be no food for the fish and they will also die. Then there will be no food for the herons, so they will die.

1 What is acid rain?

_____

2 How are frogs affected by acid rain?

_____

3 Draw **one** food chain for this habitat before it was polluted by acid rain.

4 Explain how acid rain pollution will affect the food chain.

_____

_____

Exercise 2.8 Recycling

In this exercise, you fill in a table using what you know about recycling.

Fill in the table. The first one has been done for you.

Item of rubbish	How I could recycle it
glass bottle	use it again take it to the bottle bank/recycle

Exercise 2.9 Take care of your environment

In this exercise, you will think about how you have used the environment in the past week.

1 Think about what you have done in the last week. Fill in this questionnaire.

Action	Yes	No
Did you travel in a car, bus or taxi?		
Did you throw anything away?		
Did you use electricity or burn coal or wood?		
Did you use batteries?		
Did you eat any take-away food in a polystyrene container?		
Did you use anything in a plastic container?		

If you said 'Yes' to any of these questions, you have added to pollution.

2 For the questions where you answered 'Yes', describe how your action pollutes the environment.

_____

_____

_____

3 What could you have done to pollute the environment less in the last week?

_____

_____

Language review

1 Write these words in the correct order to show how energy flows in a food chain:

> consumer   producer   Sun

_____

2 What is the difference between a predator and a prey?

_____

_____

3 Complete the spider diagrams. Use these words.

> acid rain   animals lose their habitat   bad visibility   bronchitis
> drying out of soil   fewer types of trees   global warming
> make compost   recycle   re-use   use less

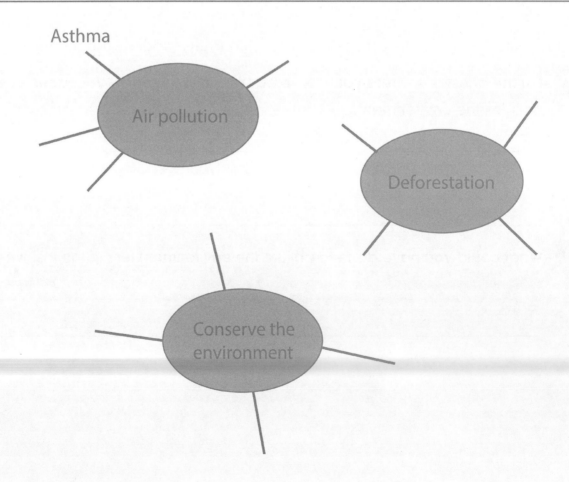

Asthma

Air pollution

Deforestation

Conserve the environment

3 Material changes

Exercise 3.1 Reversible and irreversible changes

In this exercise, you will identify reversible and irreversible changes.

1 Say whether each of these changes is reversible or irreversible:

a   melting butter in a hot pan _____

b   baking a cake _____

c   dissolving salt in water _____

d   burning wood on a fire _____

e   rusting on a tin can _____

2 How can you reverse each of these changes?

a   making a paper plane from a folded sheet of paper

_____

b   a chocolate bar melting in your pocket

_____

_____

c   water freezing to become ice

_____

_____

Exercise 3.2 Mixing and separating solids

In this exercise, you will test your knowledge about mixtures.

1 Mark each of these statements about mixtures as true (✓) or false (✗)

a   A mixture is made up of one substance.

b   A mixture is made up of more than one substance.

c   An example of a mixture is marbles and sand.

d   An example of a mixture is salt.

e   Mixtures can be separated.

f   No new substances are made when different substances are mixed together.

2 a   Draw a diagram to show a mixture of sand and marbles. Label your diagram.

b   How would you separate this mixture?

_____

_____

c   How would you separate a mixture of salt and rice?

_____

_____

Exercise 3.3 Soluble and insoluble substances

In this exercise, you will think about soluble and insoluble substances.

1 Fill in the missing words:

When a solid mixes with a liquid and becomes part of the liquid it

_____.

A solid that dissolves in a liquid is _____.

A solid that does not dissolve in a liquid is _____.

2 These are the results of an investigation where a solid is mixed with a liquid.

Observations	Mixture A	Mixture B	Mixture C
The liquid is cloudy.	✓	✗	✓
The liquid looks like before.	✗	✓	✗
The solids settled at the bottom.	✓	✗	✓
The liquid is clear.	✗	✓	✗

a   Which mixture or mixtures contained soluble substances? Name **two** ways that you know this

_____

_____

b   Which mixture or mixtures contained insoluble substances? Name **two** ways that you know this.

_____

_____

Exercise 3.4   Separating insoluble substances

In this exercise, you will think about how water can be cleaned.

Remember: even though the filtered water is now cleaner, it is still not safe to drink. It needs to be boiled or purified in a special filter to be drinkable.

1 Make a labelled drawing to show how you could use the equipment and materials in the pictures to clean water.

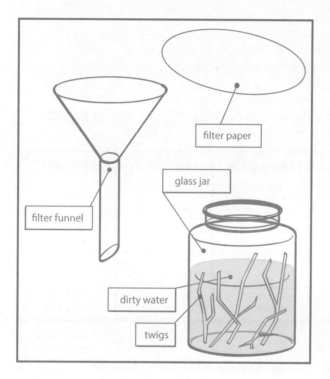

2 a   What is this method for cleaning water called?

_____

b   How does this method help clean water?

_____

_____

_____

Exercise 3.5　Solutions

In this exercise, you will test your knowledge about solutions.

Pablo added a coloured substance to water. After ten minutes, the colour was evenly spread in the water and the substance at the bottom of the beaker had disappeared.

1 **a**　Is this an example of a solution? _____

    b　Give **two** reasons for your answer.

_____

_____

2　Name the **two** parts of a solution.

_____

3　Name **one** way that you can tell if a liquid is a mixture or a pure substance.

_____

_____

_____

How can we make solids dissolve faster?

In this exercise, you will think about the factors that affect dissolving.

The picture shows a test to find out about factors that affect dissolving.

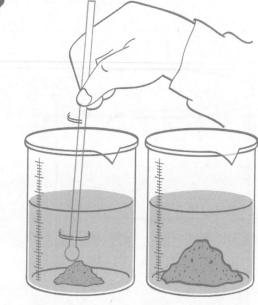

1 Which factor that affects dissolving is being tested? _____

2 Which factors are the same in both beakers?

_____

_____

3 Which factors are different in the beakers?

_____

_____

4 Which beaker is the control? _____

5 Will this be a fair test? Explain your answer.

_____

_____

_____

_____

Exercise 3.7 How does grain size affect dissolving?

In this exercise, you will consider how long it takes a substance to dissolve.

Ming and Kumei compared how long it took for different kinds of sugar to dissolve in warm water. They conducted a fair test. These are their results.

Sugar	Time to dissolve in seconds
sugar lump	90
sugar grains	45
powdered sugar	30

1 Which factor that affects dissolving did they investigate?

_____

2 What pattern can you see in their results?

_____

_____

3 What could they conclude from their investigation?

_____

_____

4 Name **three** things they must do to make their test fair.

_____

_____

_____

5 a How would their results be different if they dissolved the sugar in cold water?

_____

 b Explain why.

_____

_____

Language review

This exercise checks that you understand the scientific words used in this unit.

Choose the correct words from the box to complete the sentences. You can use words more than once.

> dissolves   filter   insoluble   irreversible   mixture
>
> pure   reversible   sieve   soluble   solute   solution
>
> solvent   suspension   uniform

1 Water boiling is a/an _____ change.

2 A tin can rusting is a/an _____ change.

3 Sugar dissolved in tea is an example of a _____ and a _____.

4 Sugar _____ when it mixes with tea and becomes part of the tea.

5 We can use a _____ to separate a _____ of gravel and sand.

6 We can separate sand and water with a _____ which lets through the water but not the sand.

7 Chalk does not dissolve in water because it is _____.

8 A mixture of flour and water is cloudy because it is a _____.

9 Sugar dissolves in tea because it is _____.

10 In a cup of tea, the tea is the _____ and the dissolved sugar is the _____.

11 We cannot see sugar dissolved in tea as the tea has a _____ appearance.

12 Water is a _____ substance but tea is a _____.

4 Forces and motion

Exercise 4.1 Mass and weight

In this exercise, you will ...

1 a Name the instrument used to measure mass.

_____

b Name the unit of mass.

_____

2 a Name the instrument used to measure weight.

_____

b Name the unit of mass.

_____

3 Class 6 measured mass and weight. Complete their table of results.
Remember to include the correct units for each measurement.

Object	Mass	Weight
brick	1	
pile of books		25
Miss Small	52	
bag of cement		400

4 a   Class 6 measured the weight of different objects with forcemeters. Read and record the measurements on the forcemeters below.

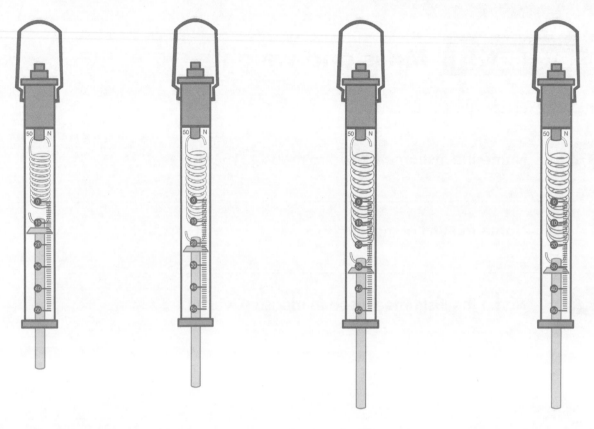

_____   _____   _____   _____

b   List the objects in order of their weight. Start with the object that has the lowest weight.

_____

5   If you pull on an object hanging from a forcemeter, would this give you an accurate reading of its weight? Say why or why not.

_____

_____

_____

In this exercise, you will use what you know about force diagrams.

1 Draw arrows to identify the direction of the forces acting in each of the pictures.

Use same length arrows if the forces are equal.

Use longer arrows to show the stronger force.

2 a In which drawings are the forces the same size?

_____

b In which drawings are the forces different sizes?

_____

In this exercise, you will consider balanced and unbalanced forces.

Look at the picture and underline the correct words to make each of the sentences true.

1 The forces shown are pushing/pulling forces.

2 The forces shown are working together/opposite forces.

3 The forces are equal/not equal.

4 The forces do/do not balance each other.

5 The bigger force is pulling to the right/left.

6 The smaller force is pulling to the right/left.

7 Movement is to the right/left.

8 Draw a force diagram to show the forces acting in the picture.

Exercise 4.4 The effects of forces

In this exercise, you will revise what you know about the effects of forces.

1 Write down how forces affect the objects shown in each picture.

a

_____

_____

b

_____

_____

c

_____

_____

d

_____

_____

2 In which drawings are the forces:

a balanced

_____ _____

b unbalanced

_____ _____

Exercise 4.5 Forces and energy

In this exercise, you will revise what you know about forces and energy.

1 Ming rides her bicycle to school.

    a   What force does she exert on the bicycle?

_____

    b   What effect does the force have on the bicycle?

_____

_____

    c   Is any work done? Say why or why not.

_____

_____

2 Mr Speed's car breaks down. He
pushes the car but it does not move.

    a   What force does he exert on the car?

_____

    b   Has any work has been done on the car? Say why or why not.

_____

_____

    c   Why does Mr Speed feel tired?

_____

_____

3 Which picture (A or B) shows that more work has been done?
Say why.

_____

_____

4 Yusef is flying a kite.

a   Where does the kite get the
energy to fly?

_____

b   What will happen if the wind
suddenly stops blowing?

_____

c   Why do you think kites are made of very light materials?

_____

_____

Exercise 4.6 Friction

In this exercise, you will think about when friction is useful, and when it is not.

1 In each situation say whether friction is useful or a problem.

Situation	Useful	Problem
a car brakes and slows down		
socks wear out		
a pencil gets blunt		
you get a blister from your shoes		
the ball you kick stops rolling		
clothes get clean when you rub them with soap		

2 Write **true** or **false** for each sentence.

a   Friction allows objects to move easily when they touch. _____

b   Friction cannot make objects start moving. _____

c   Friction stops objects from sliding away when they move.

_____

d   We produce more friction if we rub things together softly than if we rub them strongly. _____

3 Read the story and answer the questions.

Maya felt cold. She rubbed her hands together to warm them up. That didn't help much so she stuck a match to light the fire. Maya went outside to fetch more wood for a fire. She slipped and fell on the icy ground. "I must tell my brother to throw some sand on the path to the woodshed", she thought. Back inside, Maya pushed an egg the across the table by mistake. It rolled away and stopped right at the edge of the table, but didn't fall off. "That was lucky", she thought.

a   Identify the examples of friction. Say whether each example of friction is useful or a problem.

_____

_____

_____

_____

_____

b   Why did Maya want her brother to put sand on the icy path?

_____

_____

c   Why did the egg not fall off the table?

_____

_____

Exercise 4.7 Investigating friction

In this exercise, you will look at some results of an investigation.

Amina and Mira measured how far a block of wood slid down a plank covered with different materials. These are their results.

Surface of plank	Distance block moved in cm
cardboard	75
plastic wrap	120
sandpaper	25
paper towel	50

1 **a** Which surface produced the most friction?

_____

b How do you know this?

_____

c Why did this surface produce the most friction?

_____

2 **a** Which surface produced the least friction?

_____

b How do you know this?

_____

c Why did this surface produce the least friction?

_____

3 Suggest a way to reduce the friction of the block of wood on all the surfaces.

_____

_____

Exercise 4.8 Air resistance and drag

In this exercise, you will think about air resistance and parachutes.

The drawing shows two people jumping with parachutes.

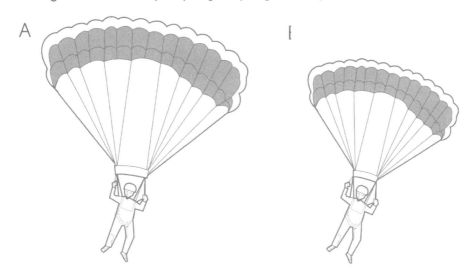

1 a Which parachute will fall faster?

_____

b Explain why.

_____

_____

2 Label the forces acting on the parachutes and show the direction in which each force acts.

3 Do you think parachutes fall faster or slower if the person or weight is heavier? How can you test your idea?

_____

_____

_____

4 When rockets are launched into space they need to escape the Earth's gravity. They use a force called thrust to do to this.

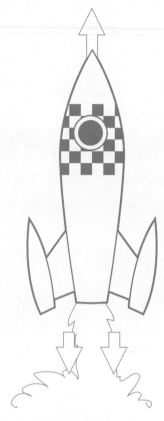

a   Label the forces acting on the rocket in the drawing.

b   Which force pushes the rocket upwards?

_____

c   Which force pulls the rocket back towards the Earth?

_____

d   When the rocket moves upwards, are the forces balanced or not? Explain your answer.

_____

_____

_____

Language review

This exercise checks that you understand the scientific words used in this unit.

Choose the words in the hot-air balloon that match the meanings listed.

weight
air resistance
work lubricate
surface area
friction
balanced
gravity
newton
mass

1 The amount of matter in an object, measured in kilograms.

_____

2 The amount of force that pulls objects towards the Earth.

_____

3 The force that pulls objects towards the Earth. _____

4 The unit used to measure forces. _____

5 Two forces of the same size that act in opposite directions on an object.

_____

6 The energy transferred when a force makes an object move.

_____

7 A force that slows things down. _____

8 When you use oil to stop moving parts of machine from getting too hot.

_____

9 The size of the outside part of an object. _____

10 The force caused by air pushing against moving objects

_____

5 Electrical conductors and insulators

Exercise 5.1 Which materials conduct electricity?

In this exercise, you will revise what you know about electrical conductors and insulators.

1 What is the difference between an electrical conductor and an electrical insulator?

_____

_____

_____

2 Identify objects 1–10 in the picture. Fill in your answers in column 1 of the table.

Identify the material that each object is made from (for example, metal, wood). Fill in your answers in column 2 of the table.

Decide whether each is an electrical conductor or an electrical insulator.

Record your answers by putting a ✓ in either column 3 or 4 of the table.

Object	Material object made from	Electrical conductor	Electrical insulator
1			
2			
3			
4			
5			
6			
7			
8			
9			
10			

Exercise 5.2 Does water conduct electricity?

In this exercise, you will revise and apply what you know about water and conduction of electricity.

1 What is pure water?

_____

_____

2 How is tap water different to pure water?

_____

_____

3 Why can plants, animals and humans conduct electricity?

_____

_____

4 Draw a sign to put up in a restaurant kitchen to warn workers never to use wet hands near electric stoves and appliances.

5 Electrical conductors and insulators

5 Jawad has just completed a 20 km run. He is very hot and sweaty.

The first thing that he does when he gets home is turn on the electric fan.
Jawad moves the fan and touches some bare wire where the plastic insulation
has worn away.

a   What has happened to Jawad?

_____

b   List the **three** factors that caused this to happen.

_____

_____

_____

Do different metals conduct electricity equally well?

In this exercise, you will apply what you know about how well different metals conduct electricity.

Tom and Aba have just finished testing some metals to see how well they conduct electricity. Here are their results.

Metal	Current measured in amps
aluminium	8.2
stainless steel	5.1
brass	8.3
steel	6.1
silver	8.0
gold	8.5
copper	8.2

1 Which **three** metals are alloys?

_____

_____

_____

2 **a** Which **five** metals would be suitable for electrical wiring?

_____

b How do you know this?

_____

3 Which metal is usually used for electrical wiring?

_____

4 Why aren't the other metals you listed in question 2 used for this purpose?

_____

_____

5 Draw a bar chart of the results using the axes below. Give your graph a heading.

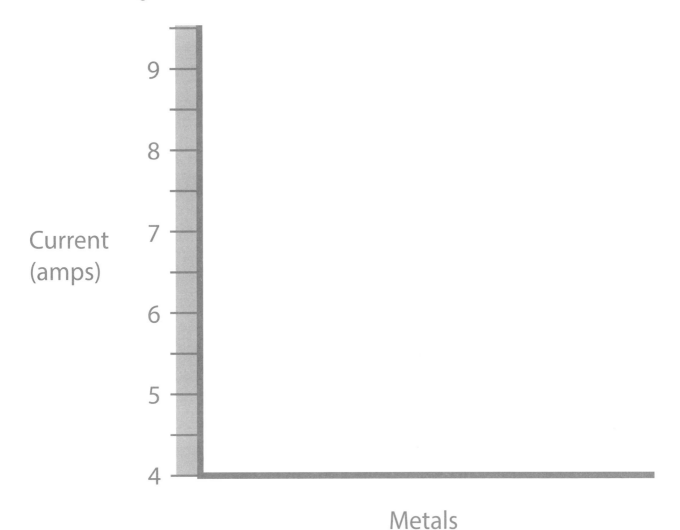

Current (amps)

9

8

7

6

5

4

Metals

In this exercise, you will use what you know about choosing the right materials for electrical systems.

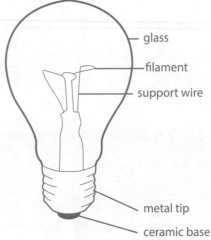

glass

filament

support wire

metal tip

ceramic base

1 a List **three** parts of the light bulb which are made of materials that conduct electricity. For each part, say why it has to conduct electricity for the bulb to work.

_____

_____

_____

b What happens to the filament when electricity flows through it?

_____

2 a Why is the base made of ceramic?

_____

b Is ceramic an electrical conductor or an electrical insulator?

_____

3 Give **two** reasons why the bulb is made of glass.

_____

_____

4 Here are four steps, labelled A to D, that you should take to replace a light bulb safely with a new one.

The steps are in the wrong order. Re-arrange them so that they are in the correct order.

A   Unscrew the old light bulb.

B   Wait for the bulb to cool down.

C   Switch the electricity off.

D   Screw in the new light bulb.

5

Lee's mother asked him to fix the iron because it was not working. Lee got an electric shock!

What has Lee forgotten to do?

_____

_____

Exercise 5.5 Circuit symbols

In this exercise, you will revise symbols for electrical components.

Match up the components on the left with their circuit symbols on the right. Draw lines linking the matching pairs.

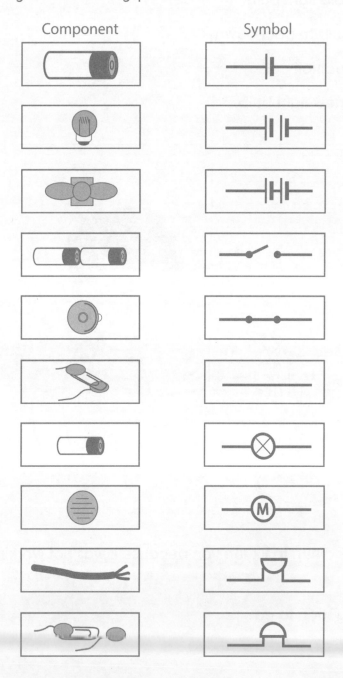

Component   Symbol

Exercise 5.6 Changing the number of components

In this exercise, you will use your knowledge about changing the number of components in a circuit to choose the correct answers to questions.

For each question (1–5), circle the correct answer from the alternatives A, B and C.

1 In which circuit will the bulb or bulbs glow brightest?

   A   a circuit with one bulb and one cell

   B   a circuit with one bulb and two cells

   C   a circuit with two bulbs and one cell

2 Why is a bulb brighter when it is powered by two cells rather than one?

   A   because the flow of electricity in the circuit is less

   B   because the flow of electricity in the circuit is the same

   C   because the flow of electricity in the circuit is greater

3 Jamil has connected two bulbs and two cells in a circuit. How can he make the bulbs dimmer (but not switched off)?

   A   replace one of the cells with a section of wire

   B   replace one of the cells with a cork

   C   replace one of the bulbs with a section of wire

4 Tracey makes a complete circuit with one bulb and three cells. The bulb lights for an instant and then goes out. Why?

   A   not enough electricity flows around the circuit

   B   too much electricity flows through the bulb

   C   the cells are flat

5 **In which circuits will the bulbs be brightest?**

A   B   C

In questions 6 and 7, you need to draw circuits using circuit symbols.

6 **Draw a circuit diagram for Jamil's circuit described in 3.**

7 **Draw a circuit diagram for Tracey's circuit described in 4.**

5 Electrical conductors and insulators

Exercise 5.7 Adding different components

In this exercise, you will use your knowledge about adding different components to a circuit.

1 Thandi and Susan want to make a circuit with a 3 V buzzer.

Write down the components they will need.

_____

_____

2 Draw the circuit diagram.

3 How could they make the buzzer sound louder?

_____

4 They want to replace the buzzer with a 6 V bell. What changes do they need to make to their circuit?

_____

_____

5 Draw the new circuit diagram.

2

5

Length and thickness of wire in a circuit

In this exercise, you will use your knowledge about the length and thickness of wire in a circuit.

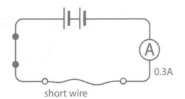

short wire · 0.3A

1 Look at the circuit diagrams. They show two circuits, one with a short wire and one with a long wire. The ammeter readings show the strength of current in amps passing through the wire.

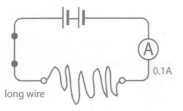

long wire · 0.1A

a   Which wire allows a stronger current to pass through?

_____

b   Explain why.

_____

2 Look at the circuit diagrams. They show two circuits, one with a thick wire and one with a thin wire. The ammeter readings show the strength of current in amps passing through the wire.

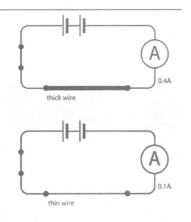

thick wire · 0.4A

thin wire · 0.1A

a   Which wire allows a stronger current to pass through?

_____

b   Explain why.

_____

Exercise 5.9 Improving Volta's battery

This exercise introduces you to John Daniell, another scientist who worked with batteries.

Read the paragraph about the British scientist called John Daniell.

Volta's pile was not good for delivering currents for a long period of time. In 1820 British scientist John Daniell developed a battery that lasted longer. His battery consisted of a large jar with a copper plate at the bottom. At the top of the jar there was a piece of zinc hanging over the copper plate. He used two different conducting solutions, one floating on the other. This meant his battery could only be used for things fixed in one place, otherwise the solutions mixed. Daniell's battery was used to power telephones and door bells for 100 years.

1 List the creative ideas that Daniell used to improve on Volta's pile.

_____

_____

2 How was Daniell's battery an improvement on Volta's battery?

_____

_____

3 What disadvantage did Daniell's battery have?

_____

_____

Language review

This exercise checks that you understand the scientific words used in this unit.

1 Fill in the correct words in these sentences. Use the words above.

> ceramic   conductor   current   electric shock   insulator
>
> battery   metal   plastic   switch   wire   switch   motor

The cover of a plug acts as an _____. The cover is made

from materials such as _____ or _____. The inside of a

plug is made of _____ which is a _____

of electricity.

You can get an _____ _____ if you touch

a bare wire when an electric _____ is flowing through it.

2 a   Label the four components 1–4 in the circuit diagram.

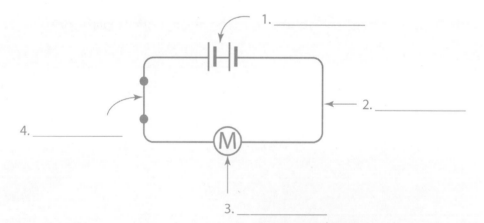

1. _____

2. _____

3. _____

4. _____

b   What could you add to the circuit to measure the current passing through it?

_____

c   In what unit is the current measured?

_____